# MARTIN LUTHER KING, JR.

## A Man and His Dream

**By Stuart A. Kallen**

Published by Abdo & Daughters, 4940 Viking Drive Suite 622, Edina, Minnesota 55435.

Library bound edition distributed by Rockbottom Books, Pentagon Tower, P.O. Box 36036, Minneapolis, Minnesota 55435.

Cover photo: Bettmann
Inside photo credits: Bettmann - pgs. 7, 19
       Black Star - pgs. 36, 44
       Archive - pg. 33
       Wide World - pg. 26

**Edited by Rosemary Wallner**

Kallen, Stuart A., 1955-
  Martin Luther King : a man and his dream / written by Stuart A. Kallen.
    p.  cm. -- (I have a dream)
  Includes bibliographical references (p) and index.
  ISBN 1-56239-256-5
  1. King, Martin Luther, Jr., 1929 - 1968--Juvenile literature. 2. Afro-Americans--Biography--Juvenile literature. 3. Civil rights movements--United States--History--20th century--Juvenile literature. [1. King, Martin Luther, Jr., 1929-1968. 2. Civil rights workers. 3. Clergy. 4. Afro-Americans--Biography.]
  I. Title. II. Series.
  E185.97.K35  1993
  323'.092--dc20         93-2296
  [B]             CIP
                   AC

# TABLE OF CONTENTS

## Chapter 1

**Growing**

**Up with**

**Jim Crow**

*"Negro infants are born into ghettos, taking their first breath of life in a social atmosphere where the fresh air of freedom is crowded out by...discrimination."* — Dr. Martin Luther King, Jr.

It was a cold, cloudy day in Atlanta, Georgia, on January 15, 1929. But on tree-lined Auburn Avenue, or "Sweet Auburn," as the King family called it, a ray of sunshine was brought into the world  In a 12-room house in one of Atlanta's most prosperous African-American neighborhoods, a son was born to Alberta and Martin Luther King. The doctor who delivered the baby boy had to slap him several times before he would cry. After that, said his proud father, Martin Luther King, Jr., "never shut up." No one imagined at the time that the tiny baby would change the world with his words and deeds.

Martin Luther King, Jr., was the first son born to Alberta and Martin King. Everyone called the older Martin Mike or Daddy King and soon everyone called Martin Jr., simply, M. L. When he was born, Martin had an older sister Willie Christine. Within a year, Martin had a younger brother, Alfred Daniel, who everyone called A. D.

The Kings were a middle class family. The part of town where they lived contained some of the largest African-American owned businesses in the United States. Their neighbors were doctors, lawyers, dentists, and businesspeople. The King children had nice clothes, new toys, and music lessons. Daddy King and his father-in-law, Adam Daniel Williams, were pastors at the Ebenezer Baptist Church. In such a nice neighborhood, the church was prosperous and the ministers were well-paid.

## LESSONS IN RACISM

*M*artin was a smart and playful child. He was happy and secure in the world of home and church that his parents provided. Then one day, when he was in first grade, Martin came home crying. When his parents asked what the matter was, he said that he had gone to play with his best friend, Bill. But Bill's mother would not let Martin play with him. Bill's parents owned a store across the street from the King home, and Martin had been friends with the boy since they were toddlers. But Bill's mother said that the two friends could not play together anymore because Bill was white and Martin was colored. (*Colored* is a term that was used to describe African-Americans until the mid-1960s.)

Martin was shocked and stunned. He never thought that he and Bill were that different. That night, Alberta and Daddy King sat down with Martin and gave him his first lesson about slavery, racism, and prejudice.

Martin's parents told their son about black Africans who were brought to the United States in chains. He was told how African-Americans were bought and sold as property and were forced to work as slaves on cotton plantations for centuries. He learned that the Civil War had brought a formal end to slavery, but Jim Crow laws kept African-Americans from equal justice and liberty. It was the Jim Crow laws that said black people and white people had to go to separate or segregated schools. This meant that African-Americans could not go to all-white colleges and were denied education that could lead to good jobs with higher pay.

From that day on, Martin had his eyes opened for signs of racism. In Atlanta, and the South in general, those signs were everywhere. Martin began to notice the signs that said "Whites Only" or "Colored" on everything from drinking fountains to barbershops. When the King family went to a bus or train station, they had to use the waiting room that was marked "Colored." If they sat in the wrong section, they could be arrested.

But Martin also noticed that many things marked "Colored" were broken, dirty, or not as good as things marked "Whites Only." If Martin was thirsty when out shopping, many times the "Colored" drinking fountain was broken. If he used the "Whites Only" drinking fountain, he could be arrested. If Daddy King took him to a soda fountain, they had to order from the "Colored" window, stand outside, and eat from a paper cup. Inside, white people sat down and ate from regular plates. It was illegal for African-Americans to eat at lunch counters in Atlanta.

*Jim Crow laws existed throughout the South. These laws kept African-Americans and white people segregated.*

At the movie theater, Martin and all African-Americans had to enter through a side door and sit on lumpy seats in the balcony. Not only was it hard to see and hear the movie from the "Colored" section, the area was never cleaned. The floor was covered with old popcorn and sticky soda pop.

One day when Martin was twelve years old, he decided to skip church and watch a parade that was taking place downtown. Although he feared a whipping if caught, he was overcome with joy when he saw the marching bands and majorettes. His joy vanished when he felt a tap on his shoulder. It was a friend of his who blurted out that Martin's grandmother had just died of a heart attack. Martin returned home in tears, certain that God was punishing him. His grandmother was like a second mother to him, and he cried himself to sleep at night for a long time after her death.

## "THE ANGRIEST I'VE EVER BEEN IN MY LIFE"

*M*artin's life began to improve when his parents enrolled him in Booker T. Washington High School. The school was much better than his other school which, because of segregation, was rundown, and had few desks, books, or teachers. The Booker T. Washington School was an experiment in quality education for African-American children–something quite unusual in the Deep South in the early 1940s.

A whole world of knowledge was opened to Martin at his new school. He learned about great African-Americans such as Frederick Douglass who had helped free black people from slavery.

He learned about Harriet Tubman, a slave who set up the Underground Railroad, an escape route for runaway slaves. Martin also studied English. His voice had changed, and his rich, deep baritone caught people's attention when he spoke.

While in the eleventh grade, Martin entered a speaking contest in Dublin, Georgia, 90 miles (144 kilometers) from Atlanta. His favorite teacher, Sarah Grace Bradley, went with him on the bus trip. Martin's speech, "The Negro and the Constitution," won him a prize in Dublin.

On the bus ride home, Mrs. Bradley and Martin talked excitedly about the day's events. At one point, the bus stopped and several white people climbed aboard. The bus was crowded, and Mrs. Bradley and Martin were the only black people sitting in bus seats. The driver stopped the bus and stood beside the two black travelers. He demanded that they give up their seats for the white passengers. When the two resisted, the driver unleashed a stream of filthy, racist language. Finally, the humiliated and angry pair gave up their seats.

As the two stood for the rest of the journey, Martin was furious. He had just won a prize for a speech about how the Constitution affected African Americans. Now it was demonstrated beyond a doubt that the Constitution did not apply to people of his race. Later he said, "That night will never leave my mind. It was the angriest I have ever been in my life."

Along with racism, Martin had other problems. Daddy King had a fierce and violent temper. He would often whip Martin for the slightest mistake. Even at the age of fifteen, Martin would receive painful and embarrassing whippings from Daddy King. This made him hate violence, in any form.

As he grew older, Martin developed a love of classical music and fancy clothes. His fondness for stylish tweed suits earned him the nickname "Tweedie." Young ladies began to notice the smooth-talking, sharp-dressed Martin and he had no trouble finding dates.

In spite of these distractions, Martin was smart enough to skip two grades. He enrolled in Morehouse College in 1944, when he was only fifteen.

To earn money for college, Martin enrolled in a work program at college. He was employed as a field hand on a tobacco farm in Connecticut. Although the work was hard, it was the first time Martin had ever left the Deep South. He loved his new freedom away from Daddy King and Jim Crow laws. Martin and his friends often went to Hartford. Hartford, like many Northern cities, was mostly integrated. This meant that blacks and whites were not separated in schools and businesses. Martin and his friends could eat in any restaurant, or attend a movie and sit anywhere they wanted to. There was still prejudice and subtle segregation in most Northern cities, but it was not nearly as bad as in the South.

When he returned to Georgia at the end of the summer, Martin had to readjust to the Jim Crow laws. As the train back home rolled into Virginia, he was led out of the dining car and seated behind a curtain to hide him from the white passengers. He said that he felt "a curtain had been dropped on his selfhood."

Martin decided he must do something to change the laws that denied black people equality. He thought of becoming a lawyer. He knew one thing, he *never* wanted to become a preacher.

## Chapter 2

**Questions**

**and**

**Answers**

*"Whatever your life's work is, do it well."* — Dr. Martin Luther King, Jr.

As Martin worked his way through his first year of college, he began to have trouble with his studies. The reason, he was surprised to find out, was that he could only read at an eighth-grade level. He was told that his reading level was low because of the inferior segregated schools he had been forced to attend. Martin felt cheated and angry. But these emotions only served to harden his desire to make good. Martin worked to improve his skills. By his second year in college, he was earning straight A's in English, sociology, history, and philosophy.

The president of Morehouse College, Dr. Benjamin Mays, was an outspoken critic of segregation. He was active in the National Association for the Advancement of Colored People (NAACP). Mays was not afraid to challenge the common beliefs about black-white relations. Mays told his students that the church should be more involved with improving the conditions of African-Americans. He said that ministers could help wipe out poverty, hunger, and prejudice.

Largely because of Dr. Mays, Martin rethought his attitudes about the church.  When home on vacation, Martin told Daddy King that he had decided to become a minister. The stern Dr. King would not let his son see the joy he felt. Instead, he commanded Martin to preach a trial sermon in the church basement the following Sunday. When Sunday arrived, the basement of the church was so crowded that the sermon had to be moved upstairs into the main chapel. Though nervous, Martin delivered his sermon with a vocal thunder that practically shook the high walls of the church. Martin's sermon was a grand success.

The next year, at the age of eighteen, Martin became *Reverend* Martin Luther King, Jr., at the Ebenezer Baptist Church. As a co-pastor at the church, he seemed older and wise beyond his years.

While studying his history books, Martin came across an essay written by Henry David Thoreau in 1849. The essay was called "Civil Disobedience." Thoreau wrote that if a law was wrong, people had a right to disobey it. That person must also be willing to go to jail. Thoreau had refused to pay taxes in the 1840s because the government allowed slavery. He was put in jail. When a friend asked him why he was in jail, Thoreau replied, "Why are you out of jail?"  Martin thought that civil disobedience could work in the struggle against Jim Crow laws and segregation.

In 1948, Martin graduated from Morehouse College with a degree in sociology.  He also wanted to get a degree in divinity—the study of religious beliefs and practices. To further his studies, he decided to attend Crozer Theological Seminary in Chester, Pennsylvania. Crozer was the best seminary in the Unites States, and it was open to black and white students. In the fall, Martin set out for Crozer to learn more about religion and to find a way to improve the world.

# THE LESSONS OF GANDHI

*A*t Crozer, Martin attended class with men and women from every part of the world, including Japan, India, China, and Europe. But Martin still distrusted white people. He felt that they were watching him all the time so they could judge him. To prove himself the perfect student, Martin always wore a suit and shiny shoes, kept his room spotless, and was never late for class.

Still, Martin sometimes encountered some nasty prejudice. One time a white student burst into his room with a gun. He threatened to shoot Martin because he was black. Other white students dragged him away. Instead of hating the gun-toting student, Martin forced himself to befriend him. Later the student publicly apologized to Martin, and the two became friends. This lesson in understanding proved to Martin that problems could be solved through peaceful means.

Martin was still searching for a method for ridding the world of prejudice. He found inspiration in the words and deeds of Mohandas Gandhi. Gandhi was a leader in India who helped the people of his country to overthrow the British government which had ruled India for many years. Gandhi taught people to organize strikes, where everybody refused to go to work. He also organized boycotts, where everybody refused to buy products made by the British government. Most importantly, he taught people to love their enemies and protest peacefully.

Martin wondered if the actions and ideals Gandhi used could work for African-Americans.

In June 1951, Martin graduated from Crozer with a bachelor of arts degree in divinity. He was the valedictorian, the head of his class, and delivered the farewell speech at the graduation ceremony. As a graduation present, Daddy King gave him a brand-new, green Chevrolet.

In the fall, Martin, aided by a large scholarship, enrolled at Boston University School of Theology, in Boston, Massachusetts. To earn a Ph.D. in theology, he studied many religions including Buddhism, Hinduism, and Judaism. The more he learned about religions, the more he believed in fighting evil through nonviolent means.

## LOVE AND MARRIAGE

*D*uring his first year at Boston University, a friend told Martin about Coretta Scott. The friend suggested Martin give her a call. He did, but Coretta wasn't too thrilled about the idea of dating a Baptist minister. She decided to have lunch with Martin anyway.

Over lunch, Martin and Coretta discussed segregation and injustice. The two found they held similar beliefs about these and many other subjects. Soon the couple were dating regularly. Within six months, Martin had asked Coretta to marry him. Coretta hesitated at first. She didn't know if she wanted to give up her career as a singer to be a minister's wife.

But love overcame doubt. After a stormy introduction to Alberta and Daddy King, the couple were married on June 18, 1953. They moved into an apartment in Boston and worked hard to finish school.

**GOING DOWN TO MONTGOMERY**

*U*pon graduation in 1954, the Kings had many job offers. Martin was offered a position at several universities, including Morehouse. Three churches had contacted him to be head minister. One of them, Dexter Avenue Baptist Church, was located in Montgomery, Alabama, close to where Coretta's parents lived. The church was one of the wealthiest in the South with a reputation for having educated ministers and important citizens. The church offered Martin the highest salary ever paid to an African-American minister in Montgomery.

Martin and Coretta were not sure they wanted to return to the South. The North offered them many more opportunities. There were no Jim Crow laws and Coretta's singing career had better possibilities in the North. And if the couple had children in the South, they would be forced to go to inferior segregated schools. Martin and Coretta remembered many bad experiences from growing up in the South. After weeks of discussion, the couple decided to go back to the South to do what they could to improve people's lives.

The segregation in Montgomery was even worse than Atlanta. Recent court decisions caused tensions to run high between black and white people. In 1954, the U. S. Supreme Court ruled that segregated schools were illegal. It was only a matter of time before Jim Crow laws were struck down. Many whites in the South were angry and refused to obey the court's decision. That week of the court's decision, Martin began preaching at Dexter Avenue Baptist Church.

Most African Americans in Montgomery worked for white people. Many were cooks, gardeners, maids, dishwashers, and drivers. Most of the black people didn't vote because they were forced to fill out long, difficult forms to register. White people had no such forms. Unlike white people, blacks also had to prove that they could read and write to vote. King was shocked about the conditions of black people in Alabama. He teamed up with another minister, Reverend Ralph Abernathy, to change the injustice.

In 1955, Martin received his doctoral degree from Boston University. Now he was *Doctor* King. He also was going to be a father. In November a child was born to Coretta and Martin. It was a girl, and they called her Yolanda. Her nickname was Yoki. Things were changing fast for the Kings. And things were changing fast in the South. Soon the whirlwind would catch up with the King family and change their lives forever.

*Chapter* **3**

## Kicking
## Jim Crow
## off
## the Bus

*"My feets is tired but my soul is rested."* — Sister Pollard, commenting on her part in the Montgomery bus boycott.

On December 1, 1955, Rosa Parks, a tailor's assistant at a Montgomery department store, was returning home from work. Her feet hurt, and she was glad to find an empty seat on the bus. The bus lurched along, stopping here and there for more passengers. At one stop, several white people boarded the bus and one white man was left standing. The bus driver turned around and ordered the black people sitting on the bus to stand up. Three black people shook their heads, but soon stood. Rosa Parks refused. Within minutes, the police dragged Rosa Parks off the bus and into a waiting police car. Soon she was in jail.

The next morning, the telephone rang at the King house. On the line was E. D. Nixon, a local leader of the NAACP. Nixon told King about the arrest of Rosa Parks, who was also a former secretary at the NAACP.

Since the Supreme Court had said that segregation was illegal, Nixon wanted to use Parks' arrest to strike down the Jim Crow laws on Montgomery's bus system.

Nixon told King about his plans for a boycott. If African-Americans stopped using the bus system in Montgomery, the bus company would lose a lot of money. Nixon wanted to join forces with the Women's Political Council (WPC) to organize a boycott. He also wanted the support of Montgomery's black ministers. King agreed to hold a meeting at the Dexter Avenue Church.

Dr. King only expected twenty ministers at the boycott meeting. He was pleasantly surprised when forty-five showed up. The WPC had printed up 35,000 leaflets to tell people of the boycott. Sixty African-American taxi drivers agreed to provide rides to boycotters for only ten cents, the price of bus fare. Dr. King was hopeful, but afraid. If the boycott failed, people would laugh at the organizers and make things even harder for the black bus riders.

In the morning, Dr. King's fears were gone when one empty bus after another rolled down his street. The sidewalks were jammed with African-Americans who refused to ride on Montgomery's buses. Some people, even elderly ones, had to walk as much as twelve miles to get to work. Some people hitchhiked, some rode mules and horses. When buses rolled up to empty bus stops, crowds gathered to cheer and jeer.

Rosa Parks was found guilty and fined $14. She refused to pay the fine and the case was appealed to a higher court. An organization named the Montgomery Improvement Council (MIC) was formed to continue the boycott. Before he knew it, Dr. King was elected to head the council. He was asked to give a speech that night at the Holt Street Baptist Church. It would be an important speech, heard by the people, the press, and maybe the entire country.

*Martin Luther King, Jr., angered many people in the South.*
*This photo shows an effigy of King hanging by its*
*neck in the city of Birmingham, Alabama.*

When Dr. King arrived at the Holt Street Church, he found that a mass of people had surrounded it. He had to park four blocks away and push through a crowd numbering over 4,000 people. Dr. King was called to the podium and his voice thundered over the crowd inside the church. Crowds in the street listened through loudspeakers. Dr. King said:

"We are here this evening to say to those who have mistreated us so long that we are tired—tired of being segregated and humiliated, tired of being kicked about by the brutal feet of oppression...

"If we are wrong, then the Supreme Court of this nation is wrong. If we are wrong, then the Constitution of the United States is wrong. If we are wrong, then God Almighty is wrong.... If we are wrong then justice is a lie."

Dr. King urged people to act peacefully and responsibly. He asked people to respond to violence by loving their enemy.

The crowd clapped and cheered wildly as Dr. King sat down. He felt that they had already won, just by coming together for the common good.

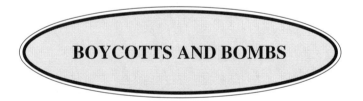

## BOYCOTTS AND BOMBS

*T*he city reacted to the boycott by saying the protesters could no longer use ten-cent taxis. The law said that it was illegal to charge less than forty-five cents for a taxi ride. With the help of another minister, Dr. King set up a private car pool. Over 300 people volunteered to use their cars to drive people around town. The system worked better than the Montgomery buses had. Some people still preferred to walk. They wanted to show the world that the times were changing. Television stations and newspapers all over the world ran stories about the courage and determination of the Montgomery protesters. Money and letters of support poured into the MIC offices from every corner of the globe.

Within three weeks of Rosa Parks' arrest, the MIC had a staff of ten and had met with city officials three times. The bus company still would not take the boycott seriously. City officials tried to spread lies about Dr. King and turn people against each other. The police began to tail him and one night he was arrested for going two miles an hour over the speed limit. They put him in jail. A group of angry people gathered outside the jail, and the frightened police quickly released Dr. King.

Support for the protest was tempered with hate mail. Dr. King received over thirty letters a day threatening him and his family. Obscene and harassing phone calls kept the phone ringing day and night. Dr. King thought about quitting the MIC. After praying for hours, he decided to continue.

Three days later the King house was firebombed. Fortunately, although terrified, Coretta and Yoki escaped unharmed. Groups of angry blacks gathered around the King house threatening violence. King told them to meet violence with nonviolence, and hatred with love. The crowd could not believe that a man whose house had just been firebombed could react in such a peaceful and loving manner.

## THE SUPREME COURT STRIKES A BLOW FOR FREEDOM

*S*everal weeks later, Dr. King and 88 other leaders were arrested for breaking an antiboycott law. In federal court, MIC lawyers asked the judge to throw out the bus segregation laws because they were not Constitutional. The judge agreed. But the Montgomery city lawyers decided to appeal the case to the U. S. Supreme Court. This is what the MIC was hoping for.

If the Supreme Court struck down Montgomery's segregation laws, then those laws would be struck down in every city, town, and village in the United States.

It usually takes at least one year for a case to reach the Supreme Court. In the meantime, Montgomery city officials tried everything they could to end the boycott. They threatened carpoolers with canceled insurance. They sued the MIC for $15,000. They harassed carpoolers as they waited at pick-up stations.

On November 13, 1956, almost one year after Rosa Parks' arrest, the Supreme Court declared Montgomery's bus segregation laws unconstitutional. Dr. King and the boycotters had won! On December 20 the law went into effect. Dr. King, Rev. Abernathy, and D. E. Nixon sat together on the first integrated bus, next to Glen Smiley, a white minister. The first battle had been won, but the war was not over.

*Chapter* **4**

# Taking
# It to
# the Streets

*"I've seen the hate on the faces of too many [bigots] in the South to want to hate myself, because every time I see it, I know that it does something to their personalities and I say to myself that hate is too great a burden to bear. I have decided to love."* — Dr. Martin Luther King, Jr.

The Montgomery bus boycott had made Dr. King an international star. His photo appeared on the cover of *Time* magazine. Almost every major U.S. magazine and newspaper reported his story.

In interviews, Dr. King outlined his program for justice for African-Americans. First, barriers to voting such as reading tests had to be eliminated. Second, federal legislation had to be enacted to insure civil rights. Third, African-Americans must start more of their own businesses and support each other in the marketplace.

Meanwhile, people in Florida and Georgia were copying the MIC's boycott example in Montgomery. Dr. King decided that African American's needed a large organization that could coordinate the fight for justice in the South.

Since black ministers were the most obvious leaders in the African-American community, Dr. King sought to recruit members from churches. His goal was to teach the methods of the "Montgomery Way" throughout the South. On January 10 and 11, 1957, the Southern Christian Leadership Council (SCLC) was born. Naturally, Dr. King was elected president of the organization.

In October 1957, the Kings' second child, Martin Luther King III, was born. Unfortunately, Dr. King had little time to spend with his young son. He was busy raising money and giving speeches for the SCLC.

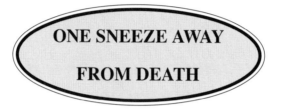

## ONE SNEEZE AWAY FROM DEATH

*I*n September 1958, Dr. King's book about the Montgomery bus boycott, *Stride Toward Freedom* was published. Demands for him to appear on radio and TV increased after the book's release. One afternoon, Dr. King was sitting in a bookstore autographing copies of his book when a mentally ill woman stabbed him with a letter opener. He was rushed to the hospital, moments away from death.

Surgeons had to remove one of Dr. King's ribs and part of his breastbone to remove the letter opener. The letter opener was centimeters from his heart. If Dr. King would of so much as sneezed, the letter opener would have pierced his heart and killed him. Later, when he was healing, Dr. King found out the woman who had stabbed him was mentally ill. He asked police to "get her healed" instead of punishing her. Sacks full of get-well cards and letters poured in. One card from an eight-year-old white girl said, "I'm very glad that you didn't sneeze."

As Dr. King looked around, he saw a lot of work that needed to be done. After discussing the matter with Coretta, he decided that he would work for the civil rights movement full-time. This meant moving back to Atlanta where the headquarters of the SCLC was located. On November 29, 1959, Dr. King preached his last sermon to the weeping congregation at Dexter Avenue Baptist Church. He told them that he could not run away from the responsibility that history had thrust upon him.

## FOUR MONTHS
## HARD LABOR

**D**r. King was a major leader of the civil rights movement. But there were many people working together in groups with the same goals. In February 1960, four black college students sat down at the lunch counter in a Woolworth's store in Greensboro, South Carolina. This was still against the law in South Carolina. The students didn't expect to be served. They wanted to call attention to prejudice.

In Atlanta, Dr. King joined a sit-in with students and was arrested. Police found that he had an unpaid parking ticket and refused to let him out of jail. A judge sentenced him to four months of hard labor in a Georgia prison camp. The sentence was outrageous. Dr. King was shackled and handcuffed like a murderer, thrown in the back of a police car, and taken 250 miles (400 kilometers) from Atlanta to Reidsville State Prison. Dr. King was terrified. Many black men had disappeared at Reidsville. The guards were vicious, and no one had any rights behind the high prison walls.

*"Sit-in" demonstrations were very common in the South. Peaceful demonstrators would often be confronted by angry people who would humiliate them by pouring liquid on their heads.*

Dr. King tried to maintain his faith, and not long after his arrest, his prayers were answered. He was immediately released and returned to Atlanta by air. Senator John F. Kennedy of Massachusetts had personally called the judge and demanded that Dr. King be released. Kennedy was running for president and needed the African-American vote. After Dr. King's release, Kennedy won the election with two-thirds of African-Americans voting for him. Kennedy appointed forty African-Americans to high posts inside the government.

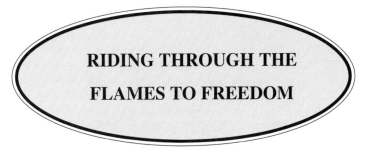

## RIDING THROUGH THE FLAMES TO FREEDOM

*L*unch counters and city buses were opening up to blacks throughout the South. But there were other places that needed to be integrated. Buses that traveled between states were still segregated, even though it was illegal. Because of this, Freedom Rides were planned across the South. On Freedom Rides, black and white students rode buses together from town to town.

The first Freedom Ride was in May 1961, when a group of students planned to ride from Washington, D.C., to New Orleans, Louisiana. Near Anniston, Alabama, a group of armed white men set the bus on fire. The Freedom Riders barely escaped with their lives. In Birmingham, police looked the other way while a gang of white men beat the Freedom Riders. A few days later, the same thing happened in Montgomery. Dr. King personally went to Montgomery to stop the violence. Robert Kennedy, the president's brother and the U. S. Attorney General, sent 400 federal troops to protect Dr. King.

The following evening, when Dr. King spoke at a meeting in Montgomery, mobs of whites set cars on fire and threw rocks through the church windows. Dr. King could not go on the Freedom Rides. He was afraid of getting arrested again because he was still on probation. He stayed on the sidelines and raised money for the cause.

That summer, a total of 350 Freedom Riders were beaten and sent to prison. In September, Robert Kennedy ordered the Interstate Commerce Commission to desegregate buses. The Freedom Riders had won.

In January the next year, the Kings had their third child, a boy named Dexter Scott.

## BATTLE IN BIRMINGHAM

*F*lush with the success of his past efforts, Dr. King decided to take on the most segregated city in the United States: Birmingham, Alabama. The city was so segregated that city officials had banned a book that showed pictures of black and white rabbits together. Over seventeen African-American churches had been bombed in the city between 1957 and 1962, earning the city the nickname "Bombingham."

The head of the police force in Birmingham was a racist named Eugene "Bull" Connor. And the governor of Alabama, George Wallace, was another well-known racist. Dr. King hoped that the protests in Birmingham would push President Kennedy and the U. S. Congress into passing a federal civil rights bill.

Dr. King knew the stage was set for a dirty and dangerous mission. He warned that some people who went to Birmingham would not come back alive. Protesters went through intense nonviolence training. Trainers cursed, spit on, pushed, and even beat the recruits. The protesters refused to fight back.

In April 1963, SCLC began protests in Birmingham. They demanded integrated lunch counters, rest rooms, and drinking fountains. They also demanded equal opportunity for jobs. Within days, hundreds of protesters were in jail. Rev. Abernathy was arrested and Dr. King was arrested for the thirteenth time. Dr. King was thrown into solitary confinement—alone in a dark, dirty jail cell. He was not allowed to talk to anyone, not even a lawyer.

**LETTER FROM THE BIRMINGHAM JAIL**

**W**hile Dr. King worried in his lonely cell, his fourth child was born, Bernice Albertine. Meanwhile, Coretta had called President Kennedy and told him of Dr. King's plight. Soon, he began to get better treatment from his jailers.

One day in his cell, Dr. King's lawyers brought him a newspaper. In the paper was a letter from eight white clergymen who criticized Dr. King. They said that since he didn't live in Birmingham, it was none of his business what happened there. They claimed that he only came to the city to cause trouble. Dr. King decided to answer the letter. Since he was not allowed pen and paper, his lawyers smuggled in a pen. Dr. King wrote the "Letter from the Birmingham Jail" on toilet paper and the edges of a newspaper.

His lawyers smuggled the letter out of the jail. Later, aides sent out nearly a million copies of the letter to churches, newspapers, and politicians. The "Letter from the Birmingham Jail" was destined to become one of the most famous essays on human rights ever written.

In the letter, Dr. King reminded the white clergymen that African-Americans had been waiting 340 years for equal rights. He stated that there were plenty of people ready to use violence to get those rights. Within a few days of the letter's publication, Dr. King and Rev. Abernathy were released from jail.

## THE CHILDREN'S CRUSADE

When Dr. King was released, he saw the protest had come to a standstill. Almost everyone was in jail. Someone suggested using college and high school students to protest. When a workshop was held, hundreds of students showed up, some as young as six years old. They demanded to march with the older kids. Dr. King was worried about their safety but he knew that children were strongly affected by racism, and that they were the hope for a future. Soon the Children's Crusade had begun.

On the morning of May 2, 1963, 1,000 children marched through Birmingham singing and clapping their hands. The police arrested more than 950 of the children.

The next day 1,000 more children marched. Bull Connor ordered fire hoses turned on the protesters. Powerful streams of water shot from the fire hoses, knocking the children to the ground. The water jets were so powerful that they ripped clothes from bodies and sent people smashing into buildings.

Then the police unleashed dozens of snarling German shepherd dogs. Behind the dogs, police clubbed and kicked the protesters.

That evening, the national news showed the bloody Birmingham protest to millions of Americans. Newspapers across the country showed photographs of children getting hosed down, beaten, and bitten on Bull Connor's orders. President Kennedy said that he was "sickened."

Two days later, thousands more gathered to march in Birmingham. When the protesters reached the police line, they knelt down to pray. Bull Connor ordered the fire hoses turned on. Silence. Again, Connor ordered the hoses turned on. Nothing. The only running water were tears rolling down the faces of some of the police and firefighters. They could no longer brutalize the marchers. The police stepped aside to let the marchers pass. Later, Dr. King wrote that for the first time, he saw the power of nonviolence. Soon, Dr. King and Birmingham city officials were sitting down together, working out ways to integrate the city.

## THE MARCH ON WASHINGTON

*T*he Children's Crusade had a powerful impact on America. Only one month after the end of the dramatic march, President Kennedy went on national television and gave a speech on civil rights. On that evening of June 11, 1963, he also introduced his new civil rights bill to the American public.

Unfortunately, many people were not happy. They were threatened by the sudden changes taking place around them. Their ways of thinking were being proven wrong and the whole world was watching.

Some chose to lash out. On the night of President Kennedy's speech, civil rights worker Medgar Evers was murdered in Mississippi by white racists. Civil rights leaders decided that even though the president was on their side, they needed strong civil rights laws to overcome the hatred. They decided that a march on Washington, D.C., would force Congress to do more.

A. Phillip Randolph organized the march. Randolph was a 74-year-old man who had been involved in civil rights work for over fifty years.

Leaders weren't sure how many people they could attract to Washington on a hot summer's day, but something needed to be done. And the morning of August 28, 1963, was hot indeed. Organizers were hoping for 100,000 people, but the press expected only 25,000 to show up. When Dr. King looked out his hotel room window that morning, he guessed about 90,000 had arrived already. When he went down to the Reflecting Pond in front of the Lincoln Memorial, Dr. King was delighted to see over 250,000 people showing their support. Over 60,000 of the people were white.

The rally was part picnic and part politics. The hot marchers cooled their feet in the giant fountain while gospel singers sang hymns and folksingers sang protest songs. The day wore on with speeches by Randolph and John Lewis, head of the Student Nonviolent Coordination Committee (SNCC). By three o'clock the crowd was hot, tired, and restless. Then Dr. King rose to the podium. As he spoke to the sea of faces, people clapped and cheered. Everyone seemed united in love and hope. Dr. King spoke:

"So I say to you today, my friends, that even though we face the difficulties of today and tomorrow, I still have a dream. It is a dream deeply rooted in the American dream that one day this nation will rise up and live out the true meaning of its creed — 'we hold these truths to be self-evident, that all men are created equal.'

*Some 200,000 people, both black and white, gathered in Washington D.C. to protest against racial inequality. Dr. Martin Luther King addressed the people with his great speech in which he said "I have a dream..."*

I have a dream that one day on the red hills of Georgia, sons of former slaves and sons of former slave owners will be able to sit down together at the table of brotherhood. I have a dream that one day, even the state of Mississippi, a state sweltering with the heat of injustice and oppression, will be transformed into an oasis of freedom and justice. I have a dream that my four little children will one day live in a nation where they will not be judged by the color of their skin but by the content of their character.

"So let freedom ring from the hilltops of New Hampshire...the mighty mountains of New York...the Alleghenies of Pennsylvania...the Rockies of Colorado...the slopes of California...Let freedom ring from Stone Mountain, Georgia...from Lookout Mountain of Tennessee...from every hill and molehill of Mississippi. From every mountainside, let freedom ring. And when this happens and when we allow freedom to ring, when we let it ring from every village and every hamlet, from every state and every city, we will be able to speed up that day when all God's children...will be able to join hands and sing the words of the old Negro spiritual: 'Free at last. Free at last. Thank God Almighty, we are free at last!'"

The crowd of 250,000 roared together as one. Tears of joy and sadness filled the eyes of everyone gathered before Dr. King. The march had shown that there was no turning back. Jim Crow and segregation were doomed, to be thrown on the dust heap of history. For that shining moment, everything had come together for the civil rights movement. People watching the march on their TVs at home did not see police swinging clubs, dogs biting children, or bloody battles in the street. They saw an organized, peaceful rally coming together under one banner of hope.

*Chapter* **5**

**Free**

**at**

**Last**

*"It is still one of the tragedies of human history that the 'children of darkness' are frequently more determined and zealous than the 'children of light.'"* — Dr. Martin Luther King, Jr.

The joy of the March on Washington was short lived. Several weeks later on September 15, an African-American church in Birmingham was bombed. There were 400 people in the church at the time. The bomb blew out the back of the church where children were putting on their choir robes. One 12-year-old girl was blinded and four other girls, ages 11 through 14 were killed. Dr. King spoke at the funeral, trying to give the mourners hope. In his own mind though, his thoughts were bleak. Some people talked of arming themselves with guns. But the father of Denise McNair, one of the murdered girls said, "I'm not for that. What good would Denise have done with a machine gun in her hand?"

Dr. King was determined to help push Kennedy's civil rights bill through Congress. His hopes were dashed on November 22, 1963, when Kennedy was murdered in Dallas, Texas.

*Dr. Martin Luther King fought hard for civil rights for all people.*

While Dr. King watched the alarming news of Kennedy's assassination, he told Coretta, "I don't think I'm going to live to be forty. This is what's going to happen to me also. I keep telling you, this is a sick nation. And I don't think I can survive either."

A week later, Lyndon Johnson, the new president, went on TV and pledged his support for the new civil rights bill. But the year ended without the bill's passage.

In January 1964, Dr. King was chosen "Man of the Year" by *Time* magazine. His picture was on the cover and he was the first African American to hold this honor. In 1963, Dr. King had traveled over 275,000 miles working for African-American rights. The *Time* Man of the Year award took its place along with 50 other awards and honors that had been given to him.

On July 2, 1964, Congress passed, and Johnson signed, the 1964 Civil Rights Act. Dr. King and other black leaders were invited to attend the ceremony where the president signed the bill. It banned discrimination because of race, religion, or sex. Federal funding could be denied any institution that discriminated against anyone. The bill established the Equal Opportunity Employment Commission that would help people get better job opportunities. Jim Crow laws were outlawed. And for the first time, the government could sue school districts that refused to integrate classes.

Although the bill was the first step, many African-Americans including Dr. King were not satisfied. The bill did not mention anything about segregated housing or acts of terror against blacks like the church bombing.

## FREEDOM SUMMER

*I*n July, Dr. King joined forces with SCLC, SNCC, and other organizations for a project called Freedom Summer. The project was started to register African-Americans to vote in the upcoming election in November. In Mississippi, only one out of two hundred black people were registered to vote. Members of the Freedom Summer meant to change that.

That summer, eight hundred college students, black and white, swept across Mississippi to start Freedom Schools. Many rural people did not even know how to read. Education was the first step to improving their lives. At the schools, people were also signed up to vote.

But working in the backwoods of Mississippi was more dangerous than marching in cities. On June 20, two white college students from New York and one black student from Mississippi disappeared. More than 200 federal agents searched the countryside looking for the men. They were finally found, shot to death and buried near Philadelphia, Mississippi. The three young men, James Chaney, Andrew Goodman, and Michael Schwerner, became heroes to the movement.

On election day, Lyndon Johnson won, with the support of most African-Americans. Most felt that Johnson was the lesser of two evils when compared with his opponent, Barry Goldwater. Goldwater had stated publicly that he thought blacks were poor only because they were lazy.

Within days of Johnson's victory, Dr. King was awarded the Nobel Peace Prize. When he accepted the award, he said he was accepting it for 22 million African-Americans.

**BLOODY SUNDAY**

**IN SELMA**

***D****r.* King refused to rest. In spite of the Civil Rights Act, in cities like Selma, Alabama, African-Americans still had to take tests to register to vote. Some tests had over one hundred pointless questions on them. Many times the white officials who gave the test could not even understand them. If African Americans forgot to dot an "i" or cross a "t," they were denied the right to vote. When Dr. King arrived in Selma in January 1965, he found people living the same way that slaves had lived on plantations over 100 years before. Some farm workers had never even seen U. S. money. They were paid in tokens that were only good for overpriced goods at a plantation store.

The sheriff of Selma, James Clark, told reporters that African-Americans couldn't pass the voting test because they weren't born smart enough. Clark had attacked people trying to register to vote. Dr. King expected Clark to order a bloody attack on marchers just as Bull Connor had done.

After trying unsuccessfully to register African-American voters, Dr. King organized a march on February 1. Over 1,000 people were arrested, filling the Selma jail. On February 18, during an evening march in Marion, a nearby town, police turned off the streetlights. In the dark, state troopers brutally beat the marchers. One man was shot trying to protect his mother and grandmother.

The SCLC decided to march 50 miles (80 kilometers) from Selma to Montgomery, the state capital. The march would last four days and draw attention to the cause. On March 7, about 525 people started down Highway 80 to Montgomery.

As they came to a bridge, they saw three rows of state troopers blocking the way. The troopers leapt into the crowd of demonstrators, stomping them and beating them with clubs. Troopers on horses plowed into the crowd; they fired teargas. Police beat the weeping, choking black people. Again, the world media splashed the violence across newspapers and TV screens. They called it Bloody Sunday.

Dr. King was in Atlanta that day. When he heard the news, he sent out telegrams to hundreds of important people asking them to join him in Selma. None could refuse. On Tuesday, they arrived.

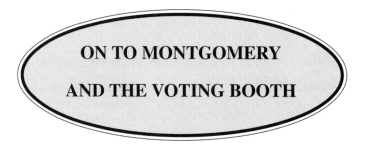

## ON TO MONTGOMERY

## AND THE VOTING BOOTH

*T*his time 1,500 people marched. When they arrived at the bridge, the troopers were waiting for them. To avoid more injury, Dr. King turned back the marchers. That night, a white mob attacked three white priests. One of them, James Reeb, died. The night after Reeb's funeral, President Johnson announced that he had sent a Voting Rights bill to Congress. He said that the civil rights movement was everyone's cause, black and white.

The next week, a judge approved the march to Montgomery. On Sunday, March 21, over 3,000 people marched down Highway 80. People from all over the country came to the march, including politicians and movie stars. White racists lined the road in places yelling insults and threats. But many poor black people who lived along the route joined in to support the marchers.

After five days, the marchers finally reached Montgomery. By then the crowd had swelled to 25,000. Ten years after Dr. King had helped start the Montgomery bus boycott at the Dexter Avenue Baptist Church, he marched past that church, still fighting for justice.

On August 6, President Johnson signed the Voting Rights Act of 1965. The act outlawed reading and writing tests used in seven southern states. It also provided federal officials to register black voters and oversee elections in order to insure fairness. Many feel that the Selma to Montgomery march forced Congress to pass the Voting Rights Act quickly. Thanks to Dr. King and thousands of others, voting barriers were permanently removed. After the act passed, black voter registration in Selma went from 333 to over 9,000. Sheriff Jim Clark was voted out of office. So was Bull Connor.

## ANGER AND DIVISION

*M*illions of people supported Dr. King's nonviolent tactics. But things were changing. Many African-Americans were tired of turning the other cheek when slapped. Even though laws were changing, attitudes were not. Passing a civil rights bill or voting act could not stop hatred and mistreatment. In August 1965, the African American neighborhood of Watts in Los Angeles was ripped apart, burned, and looted in six days of rioting. Thirty-four people were killed, 900 were injured, and over 4,000 were arrested. The cost of damage was $46 million. At the time it was the biggest and most costly riot in American history.

In addition to problems in America's cities, the United States was sinking deeper and deeper into the Vietnam War. Dr. King felt he must speak out against the violence of the war. He even offered to go to Vietnam to bring peace between that country and the United States.

This made President Johnson furious. Dr. King could no longer pick up the phone and call the president. Johnson would no longer take Dr. King's calls.

In 1967, while the United States was spending $20 billion on the war in Vietnam, vicious riots swept across America's inner cities. Boston, Detroit, Cleveland, Newark, and Cincinnati burned while police and black people shot each other in the streets. Neighborhoods looked like war zones as the National Guard patrolled streets with machine guns and jeeps. Thousands of city blocks across the country were turned into rubble.

## SHOT DOWN IN MEMPHIS

*A*frican-Americans weren't the only poor people suffering in 1967. Millions of people—black, white, red, and yellow—were living in poverty. In the South, many of the white people who were against integration lived in conditions of poverty almost as bad as many African-Americans. Dr. King decided that the solution to the problem was to bring everybody who was being hurt by poverty together under one banner. He called his idea the Poor People's Campaign, and began to organize another march to Washington, D. C.

This time, the support wasn't there. African-American groups were splintered into different factions. Some were mad at Dr. King for speaking out against the war, which shut off the support of the president. Some in the NAACP were afraid that all the poor people gathered together in one place would start a riot. Some were calling for violence. Only four years had passed since the great March on Washington, but much had changed.

Lyndon Johnson was angry at Dr. King and many other black leaders. He felt he had done more for African-Americans than any other president and where did it get him? Cities were burning, protests against the war were growing, and the very foundations of the government were shaking. In early 1968 the Poor People's Campaign was going nowhere. In the midst of it all, garbage collectors on strike in Memphis, Tennessee, called Dr. King and asked for his help. Dr. King felt he could not let them down.

On March 28, Dr. King marched with striking garbage collectors in Memphis. They were demanding decent wages and the right to organize a union. The march turned into a riot.

Dr. King felt guilty that the march had turned violent. He felt that he must organize a peaceful rally. The night before the next march, Dr. King was too depressed to even give a speech. He sent Rev. Abernathy who called and said 2,000 people had gathered to hear Dr. King. He told the crowd:

"We've got some difficult days ahead. But it doesn't matter to me now. Because I've been to the mountaintop. And I don't mind. Like anybody, I would like to live a long life....But I'm not concerned with that now. I just want to do God's will. And He's allowed me to go up to the mountain. And I've looked over. And I've seen the Promised Land. And I may not get there with you. But I want you to know tonight that we as a people will get to the Promised Land. And I'm happy tonight. I'm not worried about anything. I'm not fearing any man. Mine eyes have seen the glory of the coming of the Lord."

Dr. King was no stranger to death threats. Over fifty attempts had been made on his life in ten years. But he would not allow armed guards around him because it was against what he stood for.

*Dr. Martin Luther King, Jr.*

The next morning, Dr. King's spirits had lifted. He spent the day planning a march for the striking garbage collectors. At six o'clock, he stepped out on the second-story balcony of his hotel to get some air. It was chilly, so he turned to go into his room for his jacket. A loud pop rang out and Dr. King dropped to the ground. He had been shot in the head. At 7:05 p. m. on April 4, 1968, Dr. Martin Luther King, Jr., was dead at the age of 39.

By the next evening 100 American cities were in flames. The peace, love, and nonviolent message of Dr. King was shattered in an instant by an assassin's bullet.

On April 8, Rev. Abernathy, Coretta King, and three of her children led 19,000 people on a peaceful march through Memphis.

On April 9, over 100,000 people gathered around Ebenezer Baptist Church for the funeral of Martin Luther King, Jr. Rev. Abernathy led the services. He called the day the darkest in human history. Coretta played a tape of a speech that Dr. King had given at the church only two months earlier. For the last time, Dr. King's voice boomed through the church.

Dr. King's casket was carried on a mule cart to the cemetery. On television, 120 million people watched his last march; 50,000 marched beside him. Dr. King's tombstone was engraved with the message: FREE AT LAST, FREE AT LAST, THANK GOD ALMIGHTY I'M FREE AT LAST.

In 1983, Congress made Dr. King's birthday—January 15—a national holiday. To continue Dr. King's work, the Martin Luther King, Jr., Center for Nonviolent Studies was established in Atlanta.

In twelve years, Dr. King changed the lives of millions of African-Americans by helping them achieve basic rights. His message of peace and nonviolent change has been an inspiration to untold millions ever since. In life and in death, Dr. Martin Luther King Jr.'s dream has become the dream of all people hoping for a better world.

# GLOSSARY

**Boycott**—to cease dealing with or buying from a company in order to change their business methods. People in Montgomery organized a boycott against the city buses because of the company's discrimination against African-Americans.

**Civil disobedience**—the refusal to obey laws in order to draw attention to those laws and get the government to change them.

**Desegregate**—to stop a law or practice that separates and isolates people because of their race.

**Discrimination**—denying people housing, jobs, or equal rights because of their race, sex, religion, or skin color.

**Integrate**—to make occupancy of a place open to all races.

**Jim Crow laws**—the nickname for laws that segregated and discriminated against black people.

**Ku Klux Klan (KKK)**—a secret organization that uses violence and terror against black people and other minorities. Members of the Ku Klux Klan wear white pointy hoods over their heads and burn crosses at their meetings.

**NAACP**—the National Association for the Advancement of Colored People. The NAACP was the first national organization dedicated to expanding the rights of African-Americans.

**Nonviolent, nonviolence**—the policy or practice of refusing to act in a violent manner.

**Oppression**—the unfairly harsh exercise of authority or power.

**Plantation**—a very large farm where crops such as cotton or tobacco are grown usually using unpaid or underpaid workers.

**Prejudice**—dislike or hatred of people because of their race, sex, religion, or skin color. An unfavorable opinion formed about a person or situation without complete knowledge of the facts.

**Prosperous**—having financial success.

**Racism**—the dislike or hatred of people because of their race or ethnic background.

**Segregate**—to separate. In the South, Jim Crow laws kept black people segregated from white people.

**Sharecropper**— a farmer who pays rent on land with a portion of his or her crop. Many times the rent is equal or greater than the worth of the crop, causing the sharecropper to be very poor. Many sharecroppers in the South were not much better off than slaves.

**Sit-in**—a protest demonstration where people sit in a place for a long time. This causes the place where the sit-in is happening to shut down.

**Slavery**—the practice of forcing people to work for no pay.

**Strike**—an organized work stoppage that tries to get a business to meet worker demands. When garbage collectors in Memphis called a strike, none of the workers went to work and garbage was not picked up.

**Valedictorian**—a person who graduates at the head of his/her class.

# INDEX